Triptych

TRIPTYCH
Three Scenic Panels

MAX FRISCH

Translated from the German by Geoffrey Skelton

A HELEN AND KURT WOLFF BOOK

HARCOURT BRACE JOVANOVICH

NEW YORK AND LONDON

Library of Congress Cataloging in Publication Data

Frisch, Max, 1911–
    Triptych: Three scenic panels.
    Translation of Triptychon.
    "A Helen and Kurt Wolff book."
    I. Title.
PT2611.R814A19   1981   832'. 912   80-8747
ISBN 0–15–191157–6

Printed in the United States of America

First American edition

B C D E

TO GOTTFRIED HONEGGER

IN FRIENDSHIP

The First Panel

Characters

The widow
Her daughter
Roger
Francine
A young clergyman
Funeral guests
An invalid
A child (non-speaking)
The deceased husband (non-speaking)

The sound of a bell tolling in a cemetery chapel; then silence and light: an empty white rocking chair, otherwise nothing. The stage is blacked out, except for a bright area the size of a living room. The widow, aged about sixty, comes in, and the first funeral guest.

GUEST: Dear old Proll!

WIDOW: Yes—

GUEST: The last time I saw him was at Easter a year ago. He was in splendid shape.

WIDOW: Yes—

GUEST: How we laughed!

WIDOW: Yes—

The widow struggles against tears.

GUEST: Sophie?!

The widow pulls herself together.

GUEST: He had a good death. Not many people nowadays have the good fortune to die at home, and seventy is a good age, after all.

The widow sobs, as the funeral guest stands helplessly beside her; it takes her some time to get a grip on herself again.

WIDOW: I can't really take it in. I still see him. Sitting there in his chair. I can see him. All the time I can hear what Matthis is thinking.

The funeral guest takes a pipe from his pocket.

GUEST: I can understand that.

A young clergyman appears to one side of the scene; he turns to the audience as if to a congregation of mourners.

CLERGYMAN: "But some of them said, 'Could not this man, who opened the blind man's eyes, have done something to keep Lazarus from dying?' Jesus again sighed deeply, then he went over to the tomb. It was a cave, with a stone placed against it. Jesus said, 'Take away the stone.' Martha, the dead man's sister, said to him, 'Sir, by now there will be a stench; he has been there four days.' Jesus said, 'Did I not tell you that IF YOU HAVE FAITH YOU WILL SEE THE GLORY OF GOD?' So they removed the stone. Then Jesus looked upwards and said, 'Father, I thank thee; thou hast heard me. I knew already that thou always hearest me, but I spoke for the sake of the people standing around, that they might believe that thou didst send me.' Then he raised his voice in a great cry: 'Lazarus, come forth.' The dead man came out, his hands and feet swathed in linen bands, his face wrapped in a cloth. Jesus said, 'Loose him; let him go.' " Amen.

The playing of an organ is heard, short and not too loud, during which the deceased man comes in, wearing everyday clothes; he sits down in the white rocking chair, unnoticed by the widow and the funeral guest, and remains motionless, his eyes open.

CLERGYMAN: "Although the doors were locked, Jesus came and stood among them, saying, 'Peace be with you!' Then he said to Thomas, 'Reach your finger here; see my hands. Reach your hand here and put it into my side. Be unbelieving no longer, but believe.' Thomas said, 'My Lord and my God!' Jesus said, 'Because you have seen me you have found faith. HAPPY ARE THEY WHO NEVER SAW ME AND YET HAVE FOUND FAITH.' "

The other funeral guests come in and group themselves inside the living room. There is a certain dignity in their silence, which is maintained as they greet one another. Not all are dressed for a funeral: there is a young woman in trousers, her only token of mourning a black head scarf; a youngish man is wearing a black turtleneck sweater. They stand there, waiting. The pause continues so long that dignity begins to turn into embarrassment. At last the daughter arrives, bearing a tray with sandwiches, and the first to help himself is the man in the sweater.

ROGER: Am I hungry! Starving—though I only had breakfast two hours ago.

He takes another sandwich.

ROGER: Thanks.

The daughter moves on.

WIDOW: Haven't you got a napkin?

ROGER: I've never spoken at a funeral before.

WIDOW: I'll fetch you a napkin.

The widow goes out.

DAUGHTER: Drinks are in the garden.

The funeral guests help themselves without haste.

GUEST: Have you got a match?

Continuing to speak in a low tone:

> That young man who spoke at the cemetery—in his sweater—I must admit I found it a bit embarrassing. . . .

The young clergyman approaches Roger, who is eating.

CLERGYMAN: Where is Mrs. Proll?

ROGER: No idea.

CLERGYMAN: I want to say good-bye.

Roger wipes his fingers on his handkerchief.

ROGER: Don't we all?

For a while all the guests occupy themselves with eating, except the young clergyman, who is trying to find the widow; Roger, who has already eaten; the young woman in trousers, who is standing to one side, smoking; and the funeral guest with his pipe. The daughter returns and distributes paper napkins.

DAUGHTER: The drinks are in the garden.

The funeral guests go out slowly, each standing back to allow precedence to another. There remain: Roger and the young clergyman, and in the background, the young woman in trousers, smoking, now with an ashtray in her hand. The deceased man sits in the white rocking chair, the others unaware of him.

ROGER: Did you know him personally?

CLERGYMAN: No.

Roger lights a cigarette.

ROGER: He didn't believe in a life after death. I knew him, you know. I spoke as I'm sure he would have liked.

The young clergyman remains silent.

ROGER: I thought a great deal of old Proll—

The young woman comes forward.

FRANCINE: Here is an ashtray.

ROGER: Oh, thanks very much.

FRANCINE: It's the only one here.

Roger taps his cigarette on it.

ROGER: Do you believe in a life after death?

She stubs out her cigarette in the ashtray.

FRANCINE: I really don't know. . . .

Roger looks at her.

FRANCINE: I say I don't know.

A late funeral guest arrives, an old man using two walking sticks; he looks around the room in some embarrassment.

ROGER: I don't doubt the existence of eternity. But what does it mean? For me it is the eternity of what once existed.

The invalid approaches.

INVALID: Where is Mrs. Proll?

ROGER: She went to get a napkin.

The invalid limps off.

ROGER: All I know is that human consciousness must have a biological basis. Even a bang on the head can make me unconscious. So how can my consciousness continue to exist once my brain has been destroyed—for example, by putting a bullet through my head?. . . What I'm really saying is that death, as a biological fact, is of no great significance: all it does is confirm the laws of Nature. But there is another side of death: its mysteriousness. I'm not saying there's nothing in that—just that it remains a mystery. And even if you reject the idea of an eternal life for the individual person, something mysterious still remains, the feeling that death gives us the true picture of our lives: we live definitively.

FRANCINE: And what does that mean?

ROGER: It is *what* we have lived that counts. The various events of our lives, each one in its own place and time—there they stand, unalterable. And in that sense eternal.

The young clergyman is silent.

FRANCINE: Have you ever lost someone who was dearer to you than any other?

ROGER: Why do you ask that?

FRANCINE: Because you think so logically.

The widow comes in with a napkin.

CLERGYMAN: Mrs. Proll, I have to leave now.

The clergyman gives her his hand.

CLERGYMAN: The truth is the truth, whether your dear departed husband cared to see it or not. And he will see it, Mrs. Proll, I'm sure of that.

WIDOW: Thank you, Parson.

CLERGYMAN: A light will come, a light such as we have never seen before, and a birth without flesh; and we shall be different from what we were after our first birth, since we shall have lived. We shall feel no pain and shall no longer fear death, for we are born into eternity.

The widow accompanies the young clergyman out.

ROGER: I didn't mean to hurt anybody.

Voices in the garden.

FRANCINE: We can get drinks in the garden.

Roger and Francine go off into the garden. Only old Proll remains, in his white rocking chair. The voices in the garden are not loud but have become less inhibited. The widow returns:

WIDOW: Matthis, I know you didn't want a clergyman. How often have I heard you say that! But it couldn't be helped.

Laughter from a group in the garden.

WIDOW: They're all out in the garden now.

Silence in the garden.

WIDOW: You had a good death, Matthis. They all say that. Not many people nowadays have the good fortune to die at home. Remember your poor sister. And seventy is the Biblical age. . . . Matthis, is that what you want—that I should be afraid of you? I never treated you like an imbecile. How could you say such a thing? And in front of the doctor, too. And then you said it again to him: My wife treats me like a complete idiot. . . . Oh, Matthis!. . . What are you staring at?. . . I tell you it couldn't be helped, but you don't believe me. I told the young parson you never went to church—of course I told him that. . . . Why don't you look at me? Matthis, how cruel you can be!

Pause.

WIDOW: Oh, Matthis, my Matthis!

Pause.

WIDOW: It's a week now since you went out fishing for the last time. Exactly a week. And your shoes still everywhere, so that I find myself thinking, when it starts to rain: He'll be coming home soon. . . . You don't know what it means to be a widow. When the bells began to ring, I don't mind telling you, I felt relieved. And so did all the others.

Pause.

WIDOW: Not one of your Spanish War comrades has turned up. Perhaps they're all dead. And what can I say to these people? It was always you who did the talking. . . .

Voices in the garden.

WIDOW: It was quite right what that young parson said: death should be a warning to us, and make us look at each other daily in a spirit of love. And there I was sitting beside you the whole night long, Matthis, and suddenly you tell me you want to be alone. That's what you said. And next morning, when I brought you up a cup of tea, you were dead. It was always the way *you* wanted it.

Pause.

WIDOW: You weren't afraid of death. How often you said that! You never thought of anyone but yourself—

From the garden the sound of a glass breaking.

WIDOW: We thought there would be at least a hundred people, and it would be too cramped in here. Lucky it's not raining. . . Matthis, I'm speaking to you. . . . Matthis! What have I done?. . . Don't you recognize your own Sophie?. . . I sent for the doctor, I nursed you, Matthis, day and night. . . . I lived with you for twenty-six years, didn't I?. . . Your shoes are everywhere, and what am I to do with all your rock crystals? It's not as if they're worth much, and a whole cabinet full of them . . . . I always believed in you, Matthis, you could never bear for me to show any doubt—you would just go off again with your fishing rod. . . . I firmly believed you had put everything in order—but nothing is in order.

Another short burst of laughter from the garden.

WIDOW: They're all remembering your jokes, and you leave me here alone. . . . Oh, Matthis, when I think of everything I put up with just to make sure you would always come home, and now—you want me to be afraid of you, Matthis, you don't love me. . . . Is it my fault you had to die?. . . Matthis, you look younger now, but I can still recognize you, I knew you when you were younger, didn't I? And now you just stare in front of you, as if you didn't know me. . . . What have I done? . . . I shall die, too, some day.

The doorbell rings.

WIDOW: All of us must die.

The doorbell rings again.

WIDOW: Still, someone spoke the way you would have liked. He meant well, I think, that young man, but most of them found it embarrassing.

The daughter passes through.

WIDOW: In your will not a single affectionate word. You know that? Not one word of love . . . What did you marry me for? . . . You wanted to be left alone. That was your last word—you never bothered about what it means to be left a widow, you always talked about your mother, how she blossomed. That's what you said: blossomed. But your mother, when she became a widow, was twenty years younger than I am. . . . Matthis, I'm not complaining. You always think I'm complaining, and then you just sit there in your rocking chair, not saying a word. . . . God knows, my life has not been an easy one.

The daughter returns.

DAUGHTER: Someone has ordered a taxi.

The daughter goes into the garden.

WIDOW: Why do you stare at me like that?

The daughter's voice in the garden:

DAUGHTER: Who ordered a taxi?

WIDOW: Oh, I know your silence, Matthis, and the way you pick up your fishing rod. Without saying a word. I know, all right. And when I go to look for you because it's already dark, because I'm anxious—you're not there beside the stream. . . . Oh, the things I put up with, Matthis, just to keep us together!

Silence.

WIDOW: What have I said now—to make you grin like that? Matthis, you're grinning! . . . I didn't treat you like an imbecile, though maybe that model of yours did. Stare away! I forbade her to come to the house after the funeral. What am I supposed to do: express my sympathies to her? But of course I couldn't keep her from coming to the cemetery and standing there with just a single rose in her hand.

She weeps silently.

WIDOW: They all show compassion toward me—all except you.

She pulls herself together.

WIDOW: You want to punish me for still being alive!

She starts to sob.

WIDOW: And how could you say to me—after twenty-six years, Matthis—that you found me unattractive? That's what you said: intellectually unattractive.

The first funeral guest comes in from the garden.

GUEST: Sophie.

WIDOW: You're going already?

GUEST: My taxi's here.

He gives her his hand.

GUEST: My dear Sophie—

Withdrawing his hand:

GUEST: Look after yourself.

The funeral guest goes off.

WIDOW: Yes, that's what you said, Matthis, as I was holding your hand. Three times you said it: that you wanted to be alone. . . . I made some more tea and brought it to your bed, and you said: Thank you for the tea.

Speaking as if to a disobedient child:

Matthis, why have you got dressed again?

Voices in the garden.

WIDOW: Matthis, I must go and join the guests—it was on my account they came, after all. . . . I haven't even thanked them yet for their flowers.

She straightens her hair.

WIDOW: And there is one thing you must understand, Matthis: one doesn't start going through someone's drawers the minute he is dead. You did tell me once, I know, but with all the things one has to think of, and then the undertakers having to know immediately whether cremation or burial . . . Ilse took a great deal off my shoulders, but that was something she couldn't have known. Why did you never speak to your daughter? It was only last night I found your note, Matthis, and by then it was too late. Please try to understand. They have to make their arrangements, too. . . . What are you staring at? . . . You always made the decisions, Matthis, but there's one thing I refuse to be deprived of: my belief that we shall meet again.

The funeral guests enter in groups.

WIDOW: You are going already?

Taking leave of the widow:

WOMAN: Sophie—

MAN: Mrs. Proll—

As they go off:

MAN: Just what I was thinking. Why do we meet so seldom? There are other occasions than funerals.

A mother with a small child approaches the widow:

MOTHER: You shake hands, too, dear.

The child is unwilling.

MOTHER: What manners!

Two men come in:

FIRST: Well, just look at me! Five pounds gone within a week. You can eat as much as you want, but no carbohydrates. As much meat as you like, even bacon. But no potatoes, no bread, no starch. And swimming is no help at all.

SECOND: Bacon has the most calories.

FIRST: It's not a question of calories—

They approach the widow:

FIRST: You'll call us?

As they go off:

FIRST: I must say, your sister is very composed.

While the other funeral guests are silently taking leave of the widow, Roger and Francine come in, the last to leave the garden.

FRANCINE: Oh, no, I don't mean Swedenborg and other people like that who rely on their hallucinations. I mean, it's not as simple as you think. No human consciousness without a biological basis. How do you know? A disembodied soul, not even Plato could find a proof for that—quite right—but all the same, Plato thought it not improbable. As Bloch does, too, incidentally. There's a logic larger than the ordinary one.

The invalid approaches the widow.

INVALID: My dear Mrs. Proll.

Introducing himself:

INVALID: My name is Luchsinger. We were friends, Matthis and I, we used to row in the same boat crew, though, goodness, it was long enough ago, and then one goes on living in the same town without ever seeing each other again—

He gives her his hand.

INVALID: Mrs. Proll.

WIDOW: Thank you for your huge wreath.

INVALID: I still feel so upset.

She releases his hand.

WIDOW: I'll see you out.

The widow goes out with the invalid; only Roger and Francine still have to take leave of her.

FRANCINE: Will you hold my bag?

She gives him her handbag, unties her black head scarf, shakes out her hair, and combs it with her fingers before fastening the black scarf on her head again.

ROGER: I'll have to ask you for your name again.

FRANCINE: Francine.

ROGER: You're going into town, aren't you? I'd be glad to give you a lift. I'm going there, too.

As they go off:

ROGER: What is your thesis about?

The deceased man alone in his white rocking chair. Silence. The deceased man gets up and goes out in the other direction. The widow returns, sees the empty chair, and stops, as if frozen.

WIDOW: Matthis!

The daughter comes in with the empty glasses.

DAUGHTER: I have to be back at work at two o'clock. But I'll wash up the glasses first. . . .

The daughter goes off.

WIDOW: Matthis, where are you?

The Second Panel

Characters

The old man

The garage mechanic

Katrin

The young clergyman

The neighbour with the flute

The tramp

Xavier

Klas

The old woman

An airline pilot (non-speaking)

The convict

A young Spaniard (non-speaking)

Ilse

A man with roses

A young bank clerk

Jonas

The invalid

A child (non-speaking)

In the foreground the white rocking chair, which is empty.
The stage is wide and empty and white. Somewhere on it old
Proll is standing, with a fishing rod in his hand, as if beside a
stream; not far from him, a garage mechanic in overalls is sitting.
For a short while one hears birds twittering. Then silence again.
In the background the young clergyman appears; he looks around
as if searching for someone, then comes to a stop. The sound of
birds again, followed shortly by renewed silence. The white light
remains unchanged.

OLD MAN: I'm fishing.

MECHANIC: I can see that.

OLD MAN: Then why ask?

The old man pulls in his line, which is empty, and casts it again.

MECHANIC: There used to be birch trees here—

Katrin comes in and sits down on the white rocking chair.

KATRIN: Yes, it was here I once sat. . . . Nothing is happening
that hasn't happened before, and I'm now in my early thirties.
There's nothing more to come. I sat rocking myself in this
chair. Nothing more to come that I haven't already been
through. And I shall remain in my early thirties. What I think,
I have thought before. What I hear, I have already heard.

The sound of birds twittering.

KATRIN: It's April again.

The old man, fishing, and the garage mechanic:

MECHANIC: There used to be birch trees here, nothing but
birches. And that was a real stream. Not a canal. In my time,
that is. A stream with stones in it.

OLD MAN: That was a long time ago.

MECHANIC: You could catch trout here then.

OLD MAN: I know.

Pause.

OLD MAN: A stream with stones in it, that's right, and weeds covering the stones, so that you slipped when you tried to walk barefoot over them. And afterwards a green stain on your trousers—

He pulls in his line, which is empty.

MECHANIC: You're not catching anything.

The old man rebaits his hook, keeping silent as he does so; his manner shows him to be shortsighted.

OLD MAN: But you couldn't possibly remember the birches. When were the coachworks built? That's when the birch trees came down.

MECHANIC: I know that.

OLD MAN: How old are you, then?

MECHANIC: Forty-one.

The old man casts his line again.

OLD MAN: In those days I was still a schoolboy, and we used to catch the trout with our hands. Without a permit. That was forbidden. Only my father was allowed to catch them, with a rod. It was still a real stream then—

Pause.

MECHANIC: You should have struck then.

Pause.

OLD MAN: They all said: No new trousers for you, no new shoes, there's no meat, there's a slump going on. Only Father got sausages to eat.

The mechanic is silent.

OLD MAN: But it was long before the war that the birches were felled, and you say you're forty-one. So how can you possibly remember the birch trees and the stream?

Katrin in the white rocking chair; the young clergyman is now quite close to her; again one hears the birds twittering.

CLERGYMAN: Just listen to the birds!

Katrin, rocking herself:

KATRIN: Like in a cemetery . . . When I was a child, I used to walk through a cemetery every day, it was the shortest way to school, and in it there was a bronze bust, surrounded by privet hedges: a man with a pointed beard. Not Lenin, but some botanist. Later on I stopped being frightened of that bust: he wasn't really looking at me. I touched his eyes once with my finger: he wasn't really looking. I realized he wasn't at all interested in the way people live now.

CLERGYMAN: May I ask you something?

KATRIN: Once someone cut back the privet, to keep the black bust from being overgrown and to show the dates on the pedestal: 1875 to 1917. A man in the best years of his life. But I had the feeling he didn't want to return, even though the birds were singing.

CLERGYMAN: Why did you take your own life?

KATRIN: Because I lost my curiosity.

A man comes in; he is in his shirt sleeves and is wearing slippers; he is carrying a flute. He comes to a standstill and gazes around him, as if looking for something.

The old man, fishing, and the garage mechanic:

OLD MAN: Did you say something?

MECHANIC: No.

OLD MAN: Nor did I.

The old man pulls in his line, which is empty.

MECHANIC: Why choose here to fish?

OLD MAN: This is where I grew up. And went to school. There used to be trout here, you said so yourself. This is where we played cowboys and Indians. Where I once landed myself in prison—but that was later on. . . .

The old man casts his line again.

A young man comes in, dressed in military uniform; he has no cap and no weapon, his uniform is torn in places and stained with mud. He sees Katrin in the white rocking chair and comes to a halt some distance away.

The old man with the fishing rod and the garage mechanic:

OLD MAN: Jews! That's what my father always used to say: they buy up all the land—for who else has money when there's a slump? And they have ruined our countryside, the Jews.

MECHANIC: Well, it's true.

The man with the flute, standing to one side, begins practising.

KATRIN: Listen, Xavier, listen! Our neighbour's here, too. How awful! The dead never learn.

The man practises a difficult passage, then plays the whole melody through from the beginning, until he makes the same mistake again and breaks off.

KATRIN: Mr. Proll—!

OLD MAN: I'm fishing.

KATRIN: I'm sitting in your white chair. It's April. I've come to ask your advice—

The sound of birds twittering.

KATRIN: You'd rather not see me again, Proll?

A tramp appears and sits down on the ground, unnoticed by the others.

The old man, fishing, and the garage mechanic:

MECHANIC: Your name's Proll?

OLD MAN: Yes.

MECHANIC: Mine, too.

OLD MAN: You're also called Proll—?

He looks at the mechanic for the first time:

OLD MAN: I understand: you don't recognize me, for you never saw me as an old man. I lived longer than you did, Father.

MECHANIC: You're Matthis?

OLD MAN: People get shortsighted.

Both turn their attention back to the fishing rod.

MECHANIC: Why were you sent to prison?

OLD MAN: For evading conscription.

MECHANIC: What does that mean?

OLD MAN: Six months. Military detention, to be exact. Because I went off to Spain.

MECHANIC: Why Spain?

OLD MAN: To fight against Fascism. As it was then. You didn't live to see all that, Father.

Pause.

MECHANIC: You should have struck then!

OLD MAN: You think so?

MECHANIC: Well, of course.

The old man winds in his line, which is empty.

MECHANIC: You strike too late. That's what I was always telling you. Or too soon. You've always got your mind on other things. Or you don't fix the bait properly, though you've been shown often enough.

The garage mechanic rises:

MECHANIC: Here, give it to me!

He examines the fishing rod, the old man standing beside him like a son.

MECHANIC: How old was Mother when she died?

OLD MAN: You left her in debt, as you know. She had to go to work in a department store. Night work. Cleaning. She was a harder worker than you gave her credit for. Later she had a newsstand of her own, and went for a trip every year. A package tour to the Tirol or Venice, things like that. After your death she really blossomed. She used to say so herself: I've had more out of life since I've been a widow, she used to say.

MECHANIC: What are you using for bait?

The old man stoops down and picks up a can, which he holds out.

MECHANIC: Worms.

The garage mechanic takes out a worm and shows his son how to hold the rod while attaching the bait.

MECHANIC: Watch, now.

OLD MAN: Yes, Father.

MECHANIC: That's the way to do it.

OLD MAN: Yes, Father.

MECHANIC: And one more twist.

The garage mechanic casts the line.

MECHANIC: Isn't this my fishing rod?

OLD MAN: Yes, Father.

The tramp, crouched down alone:

TRAMP: Farther down the canal there are eleven foreign workers, but all they understand is Turkish. The boss, who skimped on the scaffolding, which was the reason it collapsed, is farther up the canal. And he doesn't understand Turkish.

CLERGYMAN: What is that supposed to mean?

TRAMP: There's no justice, Parson.

The garage mechanic, fishing, and the old man beside him:

MECHANIC: And you just up and went, leaving Mother at home—off to Spain!

OLD MAN: Yes, Father.

The garage mechanic is silent, watching the rod.

OLD MAN: Across the border on foot, then by rail as far as Lyons, where I'd been given an address. But it was a false one. I showed people my piece of paper, but there was no street of that name. Still, the taxi driver seemed to know what to do. He took me all through the town, charging nothing, and we were given something to eat and thirty French francs, a ticket to Marseilles—where I saw the sea for the first time in my life. The police in Marseilles had instructions to arrest people of our sort. We had to hang around in the harbour till we got the signal—from a policeman, in fact. It was a freighter, a French one, and next morning we landed in Valencia—

The garage mechanic pulls in the line, which is empty.

OLD MAN: Two weeks later we were at the front.

Katrin in the white rocking chair; the young man in military uniform watches her as she rocks.

XAVIER: Do you hear what I'm saying, Katrin?

KATRIN: I heard.

XAVIER: I'm talking to you, Katrin.

KATRIN: I know your lectures.

XAVIER: I don't think what I'm saying is nonsense. I mean about language. I'm not a linguist, but both of us know that the language you use is a man's language. Why do you keep quoting Sigmund Freud? Because your language doesn't exist yet—the woman's language. How can a woman express what she feels in this male syntax? When I read what women are writing these days, I can understand it word for word, which means that, when a woman wishes to express herself, she must think like a man, she's at the mercy of this syntax that men created for themselves. No sentence without a verb . . . Are you listening? . . . How I should like for once to hear what you are thinking, Katrin—you yourself, you as a woman! That's what I mean—it won't be until women discover their own language and until you see yourself as you are and express what you feel, you, Katrin, you yourself as a woman, not what Sigmund Freud or some other lord of creation has invented for you—

Katrin has stopped rocking and is looking at him:

KATRIN: Xavier, we're dead.

He does not appear to hear her.

XAVIER: Ten whole days I waited for you.

KATRIN: I have listened to what you have to say. We can say it all again, but it changes nothing, Xavier. Gradually one comes to see that. You said my intelligence was one size too small, and maybe you're right. We shouted at each other. We made up and decided to begin again, from the start: we kissed, we cooked a meal together and went to the seaside together, we lived together—

XAVIER: We made up, didn't we?

KATRIN: Yes, Xavier, we kept making up.

XAVIER: Yet all the same you ran away.

Katrin starts rocking again.

XAVIER: Why are you silent?

KATRIN: I understand now.

XAVIER: Understand what?

KATRIN: That we just keep repeating ourselves.

Katrin is no longer rocking.

KATRIN: —we are dead, Xavier.

The garage mechanic, fishing; the old man has gone, and the young clergyman is standing beside the garage mechanic.

CLERGYMAN: What's the name of this stream?

MECHANIC: Call this a stream? It was a stream once. Before the coachworks were built. Just take a look at the water. In my day you could see by looking in it whether the sky was overcast or not, what time of day it was. Is this water flowing, even? Can you tell? I can't.

Pause.

CLERGYMAN: I should like to ask you something.

MECHANIC: I was showing my son how to fish, but then off he goes, as always. I've shown him a hundred times. But he'll never learn.

CLERGYMAN: Was that your son?

MECHANIC: I'm a qualified mechanic. What can a man do when he's out of work? I got into debt renting a small filling station—

CLERGYMAN: SHELL.

MECHANIC: How did you know that?

CLERGYMAN: It's written on your back.

Pause.

CLERGYMAN: There's no time of day here.

The garage mechanic pulls in the line, which is empty.

CLERGYMAN: How did you die?

The garage mechanic casts the line again.

MECHANIC: Better ask my son.

The tramp, seated by himself:

TRAMP: Why doesn't he ask me? I died during a booze-up. Froze to death, I suppose. I was out for the count. Because I knew what lay ahead. I knew, all right. . . .

The old man, having left the garage mechanic fishing, is now standing before Katrin in the white rocking chair.

OLD MAN: Yes, Miss Schimanski, that was how you used to sit— just like that. In my chair. And sometimes you would rock it.

The sound of birds twittering.

KATRIN: It's nice here, Mr. Proll.

She rocks.

OLD MAN: You came to seek advice from an old man, and we

didn't even know each other. We were meeting for the first time.

KATRIN: The second.

OLD MAN: You said you'd been in my bookshop once before, but I hadn't noticed you. A lot of young people come to look at old books.

They regard each other.

KATRIN: You brought out some wine and two glasses.

OLD MAN: Yes.

KATRIN: You asked me what I did, how I earned my living, and I made you guess.

OLD MAN: Why didn't you want to tell me?

KATRIN: You didn't guess it.

OLD MAN: No.

KATRIN: I was glad of that.

Katrin removes her shoes.

OLD MAN: I didn't give you any advice, Katrin. I never even saw this young man. All I did was listen: Some dentist who wanted to marry you. A man of learning. That's what you said. And that you didn't love him. But a good fellow, and he knew your only reason for marrying would be so as not to have to go on working as a model. That's how I understood it: a good fellow who didn't want to turn you into an ordinary housewife. That's what you said. He knew you wanted to study.

KATRIN: Why are you looking at my feet?

OLD MAN: Because you have taken off your shoes.

KATRIN: Maybe I stayed too long.

OLD MAN: I was considering what advice to give a young lady in our society who had no wish to be a model, and you told me what you wanted to study—sociology, psychology.

Again the sound of birds twittering.

OLD MAN: Yes, Katrin Schimanski, that is just how you looked.

The tramp, sitting alone:

TRAMP: I don't hold out my hat now—the dead don't beg. They don't even curse. They don't piss, the dead don't, they don't stuff themselves with food and drink, they don't beat people, the dead don't, they don't fuck. All they do is wander through the eternity of the past and lick their stupid life stories till they're licked right away.

He titters.

TRAMP: "La mort est successive."

Seeing that nobody reacts:

TRAMP: Diderot.

To the man with the flute:

TRAMP: Hey, feller, I've met you before. On your beat. Though, to be frank, the beating was all on your side. Once on my arse, once on my head. But you were wearing a uniform then. Am I right? A blue uniform with a white belt, and that flute you're holding in your hand was a rubber truncheon.

Katrin in the white rocking chair and the old man:

KATRIN: You didn't give me any advice.

OLD MAN: No.

KATRIN: Why not?

OLD MAN: I knew you wouldn't take it, and that is also why I never wrote to you.

Katrin laughs.

KATRIN: But, Mr. Proll, you did write to me!

OLD MAN: What do you mean?

Klas in pyjamas, gathering newspapers from the floor.

KATRIN: Klas—?

He continues gathering, as if he were alone.

KATRIN: What are you doing?

KLAS: Nothing, nothing at all.

KATRIN: I thought you had already read them.

KLAS: It's nothing, I say.

KATRIN: You and your tidying!

Klas carefully bundles the newspapers together.

KATRIN: Have you nothing better to do when you're at home than go around checking whether all my bottles and tubes in the bathroom have their caps on, and shutting all the cabinet doors?

KLAS: Katrin—

KATRIN: I would have tidied up some time.

Katrin has leapt to her feet.

KLAS: What's the matter?

Katrin puts her hands over her ears.

KLAS: I'm not shouting, Katrin—

KATRIN: I get on your nerves!

KLAS: Not you, Katrin, just the hair in the toilet bowl—

KATRIN: Yes, I know!

KLAS: Then why don't you pull the chain?

KATRIN: I did pull it.

KLAS: Are you sure?

KATRIN: This is simply not true—

Klas stoops down.

KLAS: Here are your car keys.

KATRIN: Anything else?

KLAS: I'm not reproaching you, Katrin—we are living together, Katrin, and we are happy, it's only these trivial things that upset me so.

Silence.

OLD MAN: He's happy, he says.

KATRIN: I can't go on!

OLD MAN: She can't go on, she says.

Klas goes away, stooping again as he goes and picking up a brassiere as inconspicuously as possible.

KATRIN: That's how we spent our time. . . .

The sound of a toilet flushing.

OLD MAN: It's not meant as a reproach.

The man with the flute again practises the passage that always defeats him, starts from the beginning and comes once more to the difficult part, breaks off.

Katrin in the white rocking chair and the old man:

OLD MAN: I really can't remember writing to you after you were married. What did I say?

KATRIN: You gave me courage.

She rocks herself again:

KATRIN: Courage—just that . . . I can't remember the words, either. At first I thought it sad, that letter, but then it gave me courage: I ought not to sell myself. That, at any rate, was how I understood it. I should live with a man I loved, and altogether— It was a long letter, Mr. Proll, a fatherly one.

The sound of birds twittering.

OLD MAN: Now it's April again.

A nurse comes in with a wheelchair in which an old woman is sitting.

OLD WOMAN: Here. Yes, it's nice here.

The nurse goes away, leaving the old woman in the wheelchair.

Katrin in the rocking chair and the old man:

OLD MAN: And what did we talk about then?

KATRIN: Have you forgotten that, too?

OLD MAN: Did I tell you about Spain again?

The sound of birds twittering.

OLD MAN: You got a divorce; it's April once more, and you have a boy friend, I hear, a student, and you're living together— yes . . . . And why did you come to me again?

Katrin rocks herself:

KATRIN: You told me about Spain.

The old man is silent.

KATRIN: What is it like to be old, Mr. Proll? Does one want to live through it all again, again and again?

Xavier and the young clergyman:

CLERGYMAN: How did you die?

XAVIER: Tragically!

CLERGYMAN: Why do you laugh?

XAVIER: Snow falling all night, fresh snow on a frozen surface, then a thaw. Are you familiar with the mountains, Padre? We'd already heard avalanches during the morning, and we were pretty sure this steep slope wouldn't hold. I laughed when I heard a sudden noise: Boom! Not loud, just a muffled "Boom!"—as if the whole mountain were splitting. The first thing to go was the snow barrier, as we feared; snow up to our hips, you stand there as if you're stuck in cement and can't move. Like in a dream. And then the real avalanche.

CLERGYMAN: You died for your country.

XAVIER: Suffocated for it. The nine others, too, probably the whole patrol. Did you conduct the burial service?

CLERGYMAN: No.

XAVIER: The local people, who of course knew this slope well, warned us about it, and I told our captain. But all he did was roar at us: You shits, you shits! He insisted on our crossing the slope—without him—as an exercise in obedience.

Xavier gazes around.

XAVIER: Why are none of these people alive?

The tramp, all by himself, begins to recite, as if holding up something at which he is looking:

TRAMP: "Alas, poor Yorick! . . . he hath borne me on his back a thousand times; and now, how abhorred in my imagination it is! my gorge rises at it. Here hung those lips that I have kiss'd I know not how oft. Where be your gibes now? your gambols? your songs?"

He sees that nobody is listening.

TRAMP: I was listened to! I had the role of my life and twenty-seven curtain calls every evening— One morning, when I woke up, I was lying on a public bench, and the people were not clapping, just passing by. I didn't need to bow any more. Or go to rehearsals. All I needed was a piss, and that was just as well, or I'd have gone on lying there forever—then instead of later. . . . Are you listening, Parson? I'm telling how I came to die. It took thirty years. You don't die all of a sudden.

Xavier goes over to a man who is sitting and studying a map: a pilot, as if in a cockpit, wearing a blue shirt with a tie, and badges of rank on his shoulders; no cap, but earphones.

XAVIER: Were you once alive?

The pilot does not hear him.

XAVIER: I remember reading the Air Ministry report—your last conversation with the control tower, recorded on a tape: WE HAVE TROUBLE WITH THE CABIN COMPRESSION —that was eleven minutes after takeoff, then: WE HAVE FIRE ON BOARD REQUEST AN IMMEDIATE LANDING OUR NAVIGATION IS NOT OK, and so on. You were told what to do: TURN RIGHT UNTIL I SAY STOP YOU ARE AT A VERY LOW SPEED COULD YOU INCREASE SPEED AND HEAD EAST. PLEASE INCREASE SPEED IF POSSIBLE. You heard all that: ALL UNDERSTOOD, and shortly afterwards GOOD-BYE EVERYBODY. That's what you said sixteen seconds before the crash: GOOD-BYE EVERYBODY, The control tower repeated its instructions—

The pilot removes his earphones; a whistling tone is heard until he puts them on again.

XAVIER: Maybe I can show you on the map where you were at the end. . . . Incidentally, what you suspected was later confirmed. The experts, who spent months examining the wreckage, also believe there was a bomb in the rear luggage compartment, hence the loss of compression, the fire in the luggage compartment, the smoke in the cabin and later in the cockpit. I CAN'T SEE ANYTHING. Presumably you didn't obey the repeated instruction: OPEN YOUR WINDOW PLEASE. It wouldn't have helped much anyway, the experts think. The engines kept working right up to the end, but what happened to the steering they don't know—only you know that. . . . I made use of the report for my diploma. . . . Parts of a cheap altimeter were found in the wreckage, an instrument not belonging to the plane's equipment, and probably it was this that set the bomb off, when you reached three thousand meters. The plane couldn't be seen from the ground, but witnesses talked of hearing an explosion.

The pilot continues to study his map.

XAVIER: But why am I telling you all this?

The garage mechanic with the fishing rod; a convict comes in.

MECHANIC: There used to be birches standing here, and this was a real stream. The coachworks destroyed it all. They bought up the whole area. I was born here, but the Jews weren't—

He draws in his line, which is empty.

MECHANIC: You used to catch trout here.

He casts the line out again.

CONVICT: I didn't hang myself in my cell—often thought about it, but never did it. You get time off for good behaviour. After ten years. That's the usual way. And I had good behaviour, it's written in my file. Three years on the moors, six in the saw mills, till I had my accident. They said I was malingering, because it was Saturday and the doctor wanted to go sailing. They gave me an injection. This time next year I'd have got my release.

He turns to the man with the flute, who is just engaged in shaking saliva from his instrument.

CONVICT: They said I'd improved myself in those nine years, and that's the truth. I'd never have done it again. I'm sure of that, quite sure. In a year I'd have got my release—

Katrin laughs.

CONVICT: What's she got to laugh at?

Katrin in the white rocking chair and the old man, standing:

KATRIN: Yes, Mr. Proll, yes!

OLD MAN: You agree?

KATRIN: Yes, yes, call them up!

The old man makes gestures as if dialing a number.

KATRIN: That would solve it all.

The old man speaks as if into a telephone:

OLD MAN: Hello, this is Proll.

KATRIN: I've got a passport.

OLD MAN: I'll spell it: P R O L L. Right.

Katrin shows him her passport.

OLD MAN: No, young lady, not a charter flight.

KATRIN: For heaven's sake!

OLD MAN: We want a hot-air balloon.

Katrin rocks herself and laughs.

OLD MAN: She's putting me through.

KATRIN: How big should it be?

OLD MAN: I'll ask them what they've got.

KATRIN: And what colour.

The old man speaks as if into a telephone:

OLD MAN: Yes, we want a balloon. / Pardon? / Basket for two people. / Yes, I know, young lady, a hot-air balloon is unpredictable. / Pardon? / But of course, equipped with sandbags, so we can ascend again if there's a bog or a high-tension cable in the way. / Yes, I know about that: one pulls a cord when one wants to land—when the lady in the basket has had enough, for instance. *To Katrin:* She has to check how many sandbags are included. *Into the telephone:* That'll do, yes, I think it'll do. *To Katrin:* One dozen per person. *Into the telephone:* Beg pardon? / Send the bill to the shop as usual: Proll's Bookshop, 21 High Street. / That's immaterial, the main thing is a hot-air balloon. Silver-gray.

KATRIN: White!

OLD MAN: Do you have a white one?

KATRIN: White as snow.

OLD MAN: White as snow, and filled with helium or whatever you use nowadays. *To Katrin:* She has to check.

KATRIN: And where shall we fly to?

OLD MAN: That's unpredictable, she says. Depends on the wind direction. Anyway, we won't have to bother about the Easter traffic. Of course we may spend days over the Ruhr District, getting suffocated, or hovering over the Vatican gardens, which will upset the Swiss guards—

KATRIN: And who'll pull the cord?

OLD MAN: Equality of the sexes, strict equality.

KATRIN: That's agreed?

OLD MAN: There's no getting around it. You have twelve sandbags, I have twelve sandbags, one slash of the knife and we go hovering again. We each have a cord, that's quite clear, and when I have got out, let's say on account of my age, then the white balloon will soar off again into the sky: Katrin Schimanski will hover on. . . .

Katrin rocks herself.

KATRIN: Proll, I love you!

Pause.

OLD MAN: How did it continue?

Katrin puts her shoes on again.

KATRIN: I wanted to walk to the station, you didn't believe me, I really did want to vanish, balloon or no.

The sound of birds twittering.

OLD MAN: There was something else you said.

Katrin rises and kisses the old man.

KATRIN: Proll, I love you.

She stands combing her hair.

KATRIN: And what else did I say?

She stops combing and laughs.

KATRIN: I know.

She continues combing her hair.

KATRIN: I gave you my arm and said: Daddykins. And we went for a walk.

Xavier and the pilot, who sits studying his map.

XAVIER: A lot of things remained unexplained. Despite the scientific investigation of all the wreckage. For example, no one could explain why you suddenly turned to the left—twenty kilometres from the runway, which was empty, the fire brigade at the ready, as you asked. According to the radar you were still nine hundred metres up at that time. The black box wasn't recovered, since there was another explosion when you crashed. The four engines were scattered over a two-hundred-metre radius. The woods—I only saw photographs—looked as if a typhoon had struck them. According to the Air Ministry report, two thousand fragments of human flesh were recovered, none weighing more than a kilogram. Unidentifiable, of course.

The pilot removes his earphones.

XAVIER: But why am I telling you all this?

The pilot rises and looks around him.

XAVIER: Whom are you looking for?

Katrin and the old man come to a halt.

OLD MAN: There used to be birches here, and the stream was a real one. In my young days. A stream with stones in it, and weeds growing on the stones, so one slipped, walking over them in bare feet—

KATRIN: You've told me that.

OLD MAN: The coachworks stood there.

KATRIN: What stood there?

OLD MAN: The coachworks, in which all my father's hopes rested. He was incorrigible; when he was given a tip after filling up a car, he held the door for the driver and felt all was right with the world, except for the Jews.

Looking around:

OLD MAN: That man there was my father.

KATRIN: The SHELL man?

OLD MAN: And she is my mother.

The garage mechanic, having stuck his rod in the ground, is standing in front of the old woman in the wheelchair.

MECHANIC: So you're Anna.

OLD WOMAN: Yes, Stefan.

MECHANIC: You lived a long time.

OLD WOMAN: To eighty-seven.

MECHANIC: I always used to think you were delicate, Anna, that you wouldn't make it.

OLD WOMAN: Those were hard times.

MECHANIC: I left you in debt.

OLD WOMAN: Yes, Stefan.

MECHANIC: How much?

OLD WOMAN: Forget it.

MECHANIC: Our boy hasn't forgotten it.

OLD WOMAN: Because he doesn't like you: the longer he survived you, the less he liked you. Because you had always been saying: This is how it's done, watch, like this.

MECHANIC: That's the thanks one gets.

OLD WOMAN: People's attitudes have changed a lot, you know. They suddenly begin to think they were brought up wrong.

She laughs.

OLD WOMAN: Yes, Stefan, that's what happens.

MECHANIC: I used to think: Wait till the coachworks are built. And then they were built, but they had no job for me, though I was born here and am a qualified mechanic, as you know. So I thought: A filling station—

OLD WOMAN: I know.

MECHANIC: And I would have made it pay.

OLD WOMAN: Yes, Stefan.

MECHANIC: In spite of the rent money.

OLD WOMAN: You died too soon, Stefan. Before the bypass was built. And it wasn't until after the war that trade improved. I don't really understand it. It suddenly looked as if the war had been worthwhile—

The garage mechanic looks at her.

MECHANIC: So you are my widow.

OLD WOMAN: Yes, Stefan.

MECHANIC: You're better-looking than you were, Anna.

Katrin and the old man come to a halt.

OLD MAN: There's Carlos!

A young Spaniard, wearing the Basque cap of the Republican militia and an ammunition belt, is kneeling on the ground, cleaning an outmoded rifle.

OLD MAN: He's nineteen.

KATRIN: What is he doing?

OLD MAN: I survived him by thirty years. . . . During the first weeks all we had were those British rifles from the First World War, and sometimes the ammunition didn't fit. He'd been an unskilled labourer; I taught him to read and do figures.

KATRIN: You've told me that.

The young Spaniard removes the barrel.

OLD MAN: Afterwards it became my rifle.

Katrin and the old man continue their walk.

KATRIN: There's somebody who seems to know you.

*In the background appears another old man, using two walking
sticks. The invalid nods several times.*

KATRIN: He wants to speak to you.

OLD MAN: Let's go.

KATRIN: What a lot of people!

OLD MAN: It's Easter.

*The sound of bells ringing, then a Gregorian chant. It is the
Te Deum, sung by the monks of the Benedictine Abbey of St.
Maurice & St. Maur, Clervaux (Philips record A 02082 L, end of
side two). During the chanting and the ringing of the bells that
brings it to an end, all remain motionless.*

Klas, in a light-coloured overcoat:

KLAS: We're in London, Katrin, in the British Museum. You are
stroking a basalt sphinx. And then we look at the mummies.
We are alive, Katrin, and it's Easter. It's not true, Katrin, that
I'm never satisfied.

Katrin and the old man continue their walk.

KLAS: Katrin—!

The sound of a toilet flushing.

KLAS: Is that all you remember, Katrin?

The young clergyman approaches Klas.

KLAS: I know, Parson, either one loves people as they are, or
one doesn't love them at all. Those bottles and tubes she
always leaves with their caps off, the newspapers on the floor
and the hairs in the toilet bowl, I know they're trivialities.
And I did stop mentioning them, too. It's not Katrin's fault
that untidiness upsets me. Katrin is different. I did try, Parson,
but all the same she insisted on a divorce.

CLERGYMAN: May I ask you something?

KLAS: We were so happy in London. A good hotel, comfortable,
she sang in her bath, and we saw a lot as well, Scott's ship, the
explorer who froze to death near the South Pole.

CLERGYMAN: How did you die?

The tramp, sitting alone:

TRAMP: You don't die all of a sudden. . . . I ate too much, that's why I got so heavy, the body part of me, and when I stopped eating it got thin, but I knew I should never be rid of it, the body part of me. I took it along to parties, where people talked and expressed opinions. And people listened to me, though my body was bored with my opinions. It hadn't yet begun to stink, I still had my hair and all the other things a man is supposed to have, and women were in love with my air of melancholy. Evening after evening I took my bow, went in front of the curtain, bowing the body part of me. Then one morning I woke up on a public bench; the Salvation Army talked to me, and I sang Hallelujah for a bowl of soup. I had some scissors in my pocket, and continued cutting my fingernails for another thirty years.

The old woman in the wheelchair and the mechanic:

OLD WOMAN: Yes, yes, Stefan, of course.

MECHANIC: He can't even fish properly.

OLD WOMAN: That's what you always said: He'll never amount to anything. You were always so impatient with our son.

MECHANIC: And you were always shielding him.

OLD WOMAN: He got a diploma, all the same.

MECHANIC: A typographer!

OLD WOMAN: All right, Stefan, you always feel as if no one but you ever worked, the father of the family, that only you were ever unemployed—

MECHANIC: I didn't go to demonstrations.

OLD WOMAN: All the same, you were unemployed.

MECHANIC: Did I ever sing the Internationale?

OLD WOMAN: No.

MECHANIC: How did he earn his living, then?

OLD WOMAN: Later on he ran a little printing press with his comrades, and it did quite well. It was what he knew, after all. But then the press was closed down, because they'd been printing pamphlets of some kind. At that time Matt despised me, and it made me weep, but he brought me his laundry, and I cooked for him. A man must eat, after all, and how he used to eat! Without saying a word, because he despised me. But if you depend on a newsstand for your living, you have to stock what people want.

Pause.

MECHANIC: And he can't even fish properly.

Pause.

OLD WOMAN: Then after the war he had an antiquarian book-shop, and suddenly he began to do quite well. He had books there you wouldn't find in an ordinary bookshop. Do you know what an antiquarian bookshop is?

An elegant-looking man in his middle thirties is holding a bunch of long-stemmed roses; he gives the impression of being embarrassed, and he turns to the nurse, who is carrying a tray of surgical instruments.

MAN: Oh, Sister—

ILSE: Are you looking for someone?

MAN: For a vase.

ILSE: Would you mind waiting a moment?

MAN: A large one.

The old woman in the wheelchair and the mechanic:

OLD WOMAN: Ilse!

The nurse stops.

OLD WOMAN: Why don't you speak to your father?

ILSE: He doesn't need me.

OLD WOMAN: So you say.

ILSE: He never even listens to me.

OLD WOMAN: But he often went for long walks with you; I've seen photographs in his album. You still had pigtails then, Ilse, and he put his jacket around your shoulders.

ILSE: Oh, yes.

OLD WOMAN: Because it was cold; and he made a fire among the rocks, so you wouldn't freeze.

ILSE: Oh, yes.

OLD WOMAN: And you say he never listened to you?

ILSE: Oh, yes, when I was a child.

OLD WOMAN: And you have forgotten all that?

ILSE: No, Granny.

OLD WOMAN: And the bicycle? I know about that because he had run out of money again, your father, and he borrowed it from me, because you wanted a bicycle, Ilse, and you got one.

ILSE: Oh, yes.

OLD WOMAN: Aren't you being unfair?

ILSE: I wrote to him when I got engaged, and in reply he sent me a picture postcard.

OLD WOMAN: So you said.

ILSE: A picture postcard, nothing else.

OLD WOMAN: Sometimes he was like that.

ILSE: I visited his grave once, and it was exactly as it always was when I wanted to tell him something—

She looks at the old man, then turns away.

MECHANIC: She's his daughter?

OLD WOMAN: A nice child. She used to help me sometimes at the newsstand, after school; she cut the titles off the unsold newspapers, so we wouldn't be charged for them.

A young man dressed in a neat and conventional suit stands examining his fingernails and arranging his tie and his cuffs.

YOUNG MAN: Ilse.

The nurse, holding the tray of surgical instruments, stops and looks at the young man.

YOUNG MAN: Don't laugh! It's what they expect, you know: neat, but not gaudy. The white shirt's obligatory. And no long hair, obviously. In the summer, when it's hot, we're allowed to take our jackets off, but not our ties, and clean shirts every day. The sleeves mustn't be rolled up. It doesn't look good when you're dealing with customers. Customers like to see you looking like one of themselves, as if you come from a good family. A bank is based on trust.

He arranges his cuffs again.

YOUNG MAN: Ilse, as of next Monday I'll be working at the cash desk!

Katrin and the old man come to a halt.

OLD MAN: He'll never marry her. I told her that. Once the bank finds out his father-in-law's a Bolshie—they don't like that.

They move on.

The young man in the neat and conventional suit stands alone after the nurse has gone; the young clergyman approaches him.

CLERGYMAN: How did you die?

YOUNG MAN: No idea.

CLERGYMAN: And so young?

The convict in the background:

CONVICT: I shot him.

The convict comes closer.

CONVICT: You don't know me—

YOUNG MAN: No.

CONVICT: We didn't count on anyone's being in the tellers' lobby. I confessed it all. You made no resistance. I admitted that, too; you were counting bank notes and had no idea what was going on. I would have been pardoned, for good behaviour, this time next year. I'd never do such a thing again, and that's the truth, I'm sure of it.

Silence.

CONVICT: Why won't people believe me?

Silence.

CONVICT: Your name's Hubacher Erich. Aged twenty-seven. You were a Boy Scout and you went to a trade school. I know all that, because it was read out in court. And the chief clerk said you were always very conscientious and punctual. I heard all that. You were engaged to a nurse.

Pause.

CONVICT: I shot you. Yes. From behind. Yes. Now you can see me. Nine years I sat brooding about it. Nine years! And he doesn't even ask me my name.

The convict moves on.

CONVICT: Nobody knows me here. . . .

The nurse brings a vase.

MAN: Thank you, Sister, very kind of you.

The nurse moves on, the man places the vase on the floor and arranges the roses in it.

Katrin and the old man come to a halt.

KATRIN: Daddykins—

OLD MAN: What is it?

KATRIN: We're going around in circles.

The old man sees the man who is arranging the roses.

OLD MAN: So that's what he looked like, your Rosenkavalier! What else can I call him? You never mentioned his name; all I ever saw were the roses in your room: thirty-five of them, all with long stems.

The man straightens up and examines the roses.

OLD MAN: Why don't you greet each other?

The man moves away.

OLD MAN: I understand.

KATRIN: I needed a man.

OLD MAN: And a new coat.

KATRIN: You understand nothing at all, Proll, because you are a bourgeois, like all the rest who wanted to possess me—

The man and the young clergyman:

CLERGYMAN: May I ask you a question? Such lovely roses! So you know this young lady?

MAN: What do you wish to ask?

CLERGYMAN: Why don't you speak to her?

MAN: We played records together. She sat down on the carpet, then I sat down on the carpet. I don't know what we talked about—we were playing records. . . .

Katrin has again sat down in the white rocking chair. The old man stands beside her.

KATRIN: I want to sleep, I want never to have lived at all, and to know nothing—just to sleep.

She closes her eyes.

OLD MAN: But you did live, Katrin.

She is silent.

OLD MAN: Why do you close your eyes?

Xavier crosses to a young man who has a suitcase in one hand and a woman's coat over the other arm; he puts the suitcase down.

JONAS: Katrin never came to fetch her things.

He places the woman's coat on top of the suitcase.

XAVIER: Bourgeois! She got that word from you. Whenever anything didn't suit her, out she came with her "Bourgeois!" You're the only one who isn't a bourgeois, because you sit at a typewriter writing revolution.

JONAS: What are you trying to say?

XAVIER: When she walked out of our home, I waited ten whole days. And ten nights. Then I brought all her things to your place, thinking she was with you. She admired you. The way you talked about Bakunin. You explained Sigmund Freud to her, and Marcuse, and everything you wrote she took to be the truth. I thought you were having an affair. For a long time I thought that. And I didn't mind Katrin's living with you. Not in the least. But it was you who persuaded her.

JONAS: Persuaded her of what?

XAVIER: That I wanted to possess her.

JONAS: Do you think Katrin didn't know that herself?

Pause.

XAVIER: I saw her in her coffin.

JONAS: You loved her as a fashion model whose job it was to represent your idea of emancipation. If somebody other than yourself convinced her of anything, you began to doubt her intelligence; you can never believe that Katrin is able to think for herself.

XAVIER: That's what you said.

JONAS: Xavier, you're a bourgeois.

XAVIER: I saw her in her coffin—

The man with the flute is practising again.

TRAMP: "Has this fellow no feeling?"

NEIGHBOUR: What do you say?

TRAMP: I said what Hamlet, the Prince of Denmark, said when the gravedigger sang over the grave of his Ophelia.

He sings:

"In youth, when I did love, did love,
    Methought it was very sweet,
To contract, O, the time, for, ah, my behove,
    O, methought there was nothing meet."

NEIGHBOUR: You're interrupting me.

The tramp recites:

TRAMP: "Whether 'tis nobler in the mind to suffer
            The slings and arrows of outrageous fortune,
            Or to take arms against a sea of troubles,
            And by opposing end them?"

He hesitates:

            "To die: to sleep; perchance to dream—"

He has forgotten how it continues.

The old woman in the wheelchair, alone:

OLD WOMAN: Matt—

OLD MAN: Yes, Mother?

OLD WOMAN: Matt, something else has come back to me.

The old man goes to the old woman in the wheelchair.

OLD MAN: What has come back to you?

OLD WOMAN: You once said you wanted to eat something that didn't exist on earth. You kept saying it. I asked you if it was something sweet. You couldn't tell me what it was you wanted so badly, and I took you to the candy store—not the one on our corner, a candy store in town. But you just kept shaking your head, though there were so many things there that were strange even to your mother. Yes, and then you flew into a rage, because the sales clerk and I laughed at you for wanting to eat something that doesn't exist. And you were still howling and stamping your feet when we got home.

OLD MAN: I don't remember that.

OLD WOMAN: You were five years old.

The old man looks around at the garage mechanic.

OLD MAN: He goes out whenever I come in.

OLD WOMAN: Ah, well, we're a family.

The old man looks at the old woman.

OLD MAN: Yes, Mother—

OLD WOMAN: What are you trying to say?

OLD MAN: You are content with your life.

OLD WOMAN: Yes.

OLD MAN: Would you like to live again?

OLD WOMAN: Oh, no.

The old man takes hold of the wheelchair.

OLD MAN: Where do you want to go now?

OLD WOMAN: To the stream.

OLD MAN: But it isn't a stream any more—

The young clergyman and a child with a satchel and a ball:

CLERGYMAN: You're waiting for your mother and father. Maybe you ran across the street to fetch your ball. They'll be along soon to take your hand, your mother and father. I know it. What was your name? What a nice ball you've got! . . .

Xavier approaches Katrin.

XAVIER: Has that clergyman been questioning you, too?

KATRIN: He's questioning everybody. That was his job, to comfort people with the promise of a life after death, and he can't understand there's no job for him here.

She rocks herself.

XAVIER: Katrin—!

He waits until she stops rocking.

KATRIN: We just keep on telling each other what we have already said. One comes to realize it gradually, Xavier: there's nothing more to come.

She rocks herself again.

XAVIER: Ten whole days I waited. Then I took your things to Jonas's place, thinking you would be with him. Why didn't you let me know? Then I heard you were working at Proll's bookshop—

Katrin is silent.

XAVIER: I'm sorry for old Proll. The only man who sees you as an individual, and in the end you lead him astray, too. At heart you think him disgusting—but you make an effort, because you need someone who considers you intelligent, and Mr. Proll, I can well believe it, makes an effort, too; he's old, and he's kind to you because he's old and is afraid of being left alone.

Katrin stops rocking.

XAVIER: Oh, Katrin!

KATRIN: That's what you said to me on the station platform, as I stood there crying, and I thought about what you said, Xavier, all night long—

The man with the flute starts to practise again.

KATRIN: He won't close his window. I shouted to him during the night: Can't you please shut your window?

The man with the flute continues practising, until he comes to the difficult passage, and breaks off.

XAVIER: Since when have you been collecting sleeping pills?

The tramp, sitting alone:

TRAMP: Now I remember.

He recites:

TRAMP: "No more; and by a sleep to say we end
         The heart-ache, and the thousand natural shocks
         That flesh is heir to, 'tis a consummation
         Devoutly to be wished. To die, — to sleep; —
         To sleep! perchance to dream: ay, there's the rub;
         For in that sleep of death what dreams may come?"

Katrin in the rocking chair and Xavier:

XAVIER: I looked at you in your coffin.

KATRIN: Did you?

XAVIER: A whole hour.

KATRIN: Did you remember how I used to laugh at your lectures in the kitchen, while you were washing up, and how you once slapped my face because I had slapped yours, and how childishly I behaved on the platform?

XAVIER: I spoke to you.

KATRIN: I didn't hear.

She rocks herself again.

XAVIER: Oh, Katrin!

She is not rocking now.

KATRIN: So you looked at me—for a full hour—with my sharp alabaster nose and white lips that seemed almost to be smiling, and these hands which had suddenly become virginal again.

XAVIER: I didn't kiss you.

KATRIN: Thanks.

XAVIER: What do you mean?

She is rocking again.

KATRIN: We don't hurt each other any more, Xavier, we're dead, Xavier, and what remains is that we didn't understand one another.

The old man with the fishing rod; the invalid, who previously greeted him with nods, is standing beside him.

INVALID: I know, I know, I should have come along earlier. I always meant to. We were friends once. Then suddenly it's too late. Yet I often thought about you. Whether you believe it or not. It was a great shock when I read one day that you were dead. I even used to dream about you—

The old man looks at him.

INVALID: Why didn't we ever have it out together?

The young clergyman returns.

CLERGYMAN: The pilot has found his child!

He stands there alone.

The old man with the fishing rod and the invalid:

INVALID: Matthis Proll—

OLD MAN: Yes?

INVALID: You haven't changed at all: you stand there fishing, while I wait around, hoping for a reconciliation. . . . We were in the same boat crew. You helped me with my diploma. When you returned from your beloved Spain, I let you live for six months in my house.

OLD MAN: I was grateful for that.

INVALID: Well, then.

The old man looks at his line.

INVALID: I had a talk with Sophie, that was after your funeral, and I spoke quite frankly. It's true I did now and again say Proll was a Stalinist and would always be a Stalinist.

OLD MAN: I never knew that.

INVALID: But it did damage your business.

The old man pulls in his line, which is empty.

INVALID: Are you listening to me?

The old man baits his hook.

OLD MAN: When was that uprising in Hungary?

INVALID: 1956.

OLD MAN: A long time ago.

INVALID: Matthis, that's what I mean—

OLD MAN: You became a company director?

INVALID: What has that got to do with it?

OLD MAN: Otherwise I know little about you. Somebody did mention later that you were using two walking sticks.

INVALID: Why didn't you ever phone me?

OLD MAN: Arthritis, is it?

INVALID: After all, you did know I was still alive, and we were living in the same town.

The old man is tinkering with his line.

INVALID: Sophie understood me, I think. Those were difficult times. Then. I didn't call you when your telephone was being tapped, that's true. But you didn't call me, either. Not once. You could have called me from a public phone. Please try to understand, I had the feeling that you despised me. And, incidentally, I did once write you a letter, though I didn't send it. I was also in your little bookshop once—

OLD MAN: When?

INVALID: You weren't there at the time.

OLD MAN: Did you find what you were looking for?

He throws out his line again.

INVALID: I wanted to ask your pardon, Matthis. I thought two intelligent men like ourselves, two grownup men—we can at least talk to each other, we were friends once—

The old man is looking at his line.

INVALID: I don't mean anything to you at all!

Katrin in the white rocking chair, and Jonas, who comes in with her coat and her suitcase, which he puts down beside her.

JONAS: Xavier has brought your things.

He lays the coat on top of the suitcase.

KATRIN: Did your revolution ever take place?

JONAS: I don't believe so.

KATRIN: You were out on the barricades.

JONAS: No.

KATRIN: But you're bleeding.

JONAS: They were shooting into the crowd.

The man with the flute starts practising again, but breaks off when he sees the clergyman beside him.

NEIGHBOUR: Does my practising disturb you?

CLERGYMAN: Nothing succeeds without practice.

NEIGHBOUR: Not all my neighbours are as understanding as you, Parson. Why don't I close the window? It's just that one sometimes forgets.

He starts to play again.

NEIGHBOUR: This is a difficult passage.

CLERGYMAN: May I ask you something?

NEIGHBOUR: I haven't much talent, Parson, I know that, but a man needs a hobby. Working all day long, sometimes nights, too. I wasn't allowed to practise in the hospital.

CLERGYMAN: I understand.

NEIGHBOUR: I'm convalescing.

CLERGYMAN: I understand.

NEIGHBOUR: But it's not cancer, otherwise they wouldn't have allowed me home. Now I can practise again.

CLERGYMAN: Do you believe in God?

NEIGHBOUR: A colleague of yours was also asking me that. A Catholic. It was a Catholic hospital.

CLERGYMAN: There is only One God.

NEIGHBOUR: That's what your colleague said, too. . . . You know, Parson: when I became a policeman—first I took a course in architectural drawing, but there were no jobs to be had, so then I took up handball, I was a good handball player, and then I saw this poster: a safe, manly occupation for healthy young men. My fiancée thought I was disgusting to be thinking of my pension at the age of twenty-six. Today we're glad of it, I can tell you, really glad of it.

He shakes saliva from his flute.

NEIGHBOUR: God. I used to say: There must be something like that. And I believe it, too. Some order, that's what's needed. I'm an auxiliary, I don't give orders to shoot, Parson. That's all in the rule book. And when things suddenly start happening, one appreciates being given orders. . . . Whether it's the right ones who get killed at such times, no one can tell. Only God knows that. That's as far as I'd go.

The tramp, sitting alone:

TRAMP: IT'S A PITY ABOUT MANKIND. Strindberg. IT'S A PITY ABOUT MANKIND.

The old man with the fishing rod; Xavier is watching.

OLD MAN: Katrin has told me about you.

He pulls in his line, which is empty.

XAVIER: When was the last time you caught anything?

The old man baits his hook.

XAVIER: At school I was once sent out of the room and made to stand in the corridor for the rest of the lesson, because I asked whether there were any fish in the river Styx. I meant it purely as a factual question, but the whole class laughed, and the teacher felt insulted, for he didn't know, either.

OLD MAN: There are none.

He casts his line again.

OLD MAN: That time you came to the bookshop to see whether Katrin was really working there, whether she knew her way through the catalogue, could look up ANARCHISM, for instance—

XAVIER: So you remember that?

OLD MAN: You wanted to ask me something.

XAVIER: Yes.

OLD MAN: What was it?

XAVIER: And suddenly you were gone.

OLD MAN: Suddenly, for the first time, I had the feeling that
Katrin found me disgusting. That's the sort of thing one
doesn't forget.

Pause.

XAVIER: Did you consider Katrin intelligent?

OLD MAN: Was that what you wanted to ask?

The old man regards his line.

XAVIER: Mr. Proll, were you ever alive?

OLD MAN: Oh, yes—now and again . . . But here there is nothing
to look forward to. That's the difference. For instance, when
you came into my shop—I don't know what you hoped to
achieve. Maybe you didn't know yourself. You were curious
to see how Katrin would behave, how you yourself would
behave. You were looking for something to happen that
morning you came to the shop. A miracle, or no miracle,
but something at least. All one's life one spends in constant
expectation of something, from one hour to the next. . . .
Here there is no longer expectation; there's no fear, either, no
future, and that's why it all seems so trivial, when it has come
to an end for all time.

The old man looks at Xavier.

OLD MAN: Katrin loved you.

The young clergyman approaches the tramp.

CLERGYMAN: The pilot has found his child!

TRAMP: Hallelujah.

CLERGYMAN: Why don't you look?

TRAMP: I can imagine it.

CLERGYMAN: Take a look!

The tramp turns and looks.

TRAMP: Just as Mummy filmed them.

CLERGYMAN: Aren't they happy?

TRAMP: Now the child throws, now Daddy catches, now Daddy throws, now the child catches—no, he misses, but Daddy fetches the ball and throws again, now the child catches. And Daddy claps his hands. Now the child throws again. But too low, and Daddy has to stoop. Exactly as it used to be! And now the child catches, now it throws, now Daddy catches again.

He is no longer looking:

TRAMP: Kodachrome.

CLERGYMAN: What did you say?

TRAMP: They're not playing ball, Parson, once they were playing ball, and what has been can't be altered, and that is eternity.

Katrin in the white rocking chair, and Jonas, who is standing, looking around him:

KATRIN: Where do you want to go, Jonas? Here you'll meet nobody you don't know already. Bakunin and all the rest of them, you'll never meet them—

Jonas looks at Katrin.

JONAS: I dreamed this once: a place I didn't know—just like this—and whom did I meet? Katrin Schimanski, and you seemed very odd. You knew everything. I wasn't at all afraid of you. For the first time. And there was really nothing to say. I told you I loved you. Not in so many words, but you understood. Why I didn't want you to come and live with me, no mention of that. We were simply here in this place, and I could see how pleased you were. You said: We can't touch each other. But you were tender in a way I'd never seen. . . . It was a long and rather complicated dream, but I know I never felt frightened. All so easy. It was only when I woke up that I remembered Katrin Schimanski was dead. A year ago. That's why you said: We can't touch each other.

The man with the flute, in shirt sleeves and slippers, practises his melody again, until he makes his usual mistake. The tramp, sitting on the ground far away from him, whistles the melody correctly. The man looks at the tramp.

TRAMP: What a patient fellow you are!

The man with the flute tries again.

The old man alone with his fishing rod; he watches his line, while the young Spaniard from the militia loads his clean rifle.

OLD MAN: So you've loaded the rifle, Carlos, our British rifle. I was there when you died, November '37. Some time later I visited your village again, our billet there, but there's nothing left to see. They still have a photograph of you, a little one, now very faded: sitting just as you are now.

The old man looks at the young Spaniard.

OLD MAN: You believe in Stalin.

He looks again at his line.

OLD MAN: I survived you by thirty-two years, but your sisters still recognized me, and so did your younger brother, who buried you. A lot of your comrades were shot dead after losing their rifles. Others died in prison, some of them under torture.

Jonas is standing alone.

JONAS: The revolution will come. The minority know that, the majority confirm it with their fear. The coming revolution will make us immortal, even if we don't live to see it—

The tramp, sitting alone:

TRAMP: My memory is dried up, the role of my life is now being played by others, and the dead are slowly growing weary of themselves.

The young clergyman, standing alone:

CLERGYMAN: A light will come, a light such as we have never seen before, and a birth without flesh; and we shall be different from what we were after our first birth, since we shall have lived. We shall feel no pain and shall no longer fear death, for we are born into eternity.

Katrin alone in the white rocking chair; beside her the suitcase with her coat on it, on the other side the vase with the roses.

KATRIN: Daddykins!

OLD MAN: I'm fishing.

KATRIN: Eternity is banal.

The sound of birds twittering.

KATRIN: And now it's April again.

The Third Panel

Characters

Roger
Francine
A news vendor
A gendarme (non-speaking)

A marble bench in a public place, nothing else visible. Night. Francine and Roger are sitting on the bench in the radius of light of an overhanging street lamp.

ROGER: Say something, Francine!

She is silent.

ROGER: There, right in front of us, the black Renaissance, the park railings. I haven't forgotten those, with their gilded, pointed spikes. Yet I would have sworn the bench was cast iron and wood. And those traffic lights in the distance: silence on red, a sudden roar on green—

He takes a cigarette and lights it.

ROGER: Yes, Francine, it was here.

The sound of traffic in the distance, then silence. The traffic lights, which cannot be seen, change every fifty seconds. It is obviously a crossing where a big street meets a smaller one; in one direction the volume of traffic is large, and the sound of a great many cars can be heard when the light turns green, occasionally the harsh roar of a bus; in the other direction the cars are isolated, and the noise is not always the same every fifty seconds; the first phase lasts some time (up to seven seconds), the second phase, following after fifty seconds, lasts only a short while.

FRANCINE: You don't have to accompany me, Roger.

ROGER: That's what you said.

FRANCINE: There are times, Roger, when I hate you, but I shall never forget, Roger, that I once loved you very much.

ROGER: That's what you said.

FRANCINE: We should never have lived together.

Pause.

FRANCINE: At this time of night there are no trains. What is the point of going to the station so early? I can't see why you shouldn't come back to the hotel and rest until it's time for your train.

ROGER: That's what you said—

He smokes:

ROGER: — and I decided it would be better to go, not to the
hotel with you, but to the station. And after that we never
saw each other again.

He stamps out his cigarette.

ROGER: Your family looks on me more or less as your
murderer. At any rate, that's what I hear indirectly. Others
don't go quite that far. But they felt, our friends did, the need
to take sides. The ones who adored Francine had to condemn
me. When I mentioned your name, their silence was sometimes
quite comical. I never found out how much they really knew
about our relationship. They're tactful people, most of them.
But at the time I lost several friends. I was told you wouldn't
allow my name to be mentioned in your presence—

She takes a cigarette.

ROGER: This morning, just after I arrived, I met Madame
Tailleur, or whatever she calls herself, that friend of yours. I
wouldn't have recognized her, a ghost from the past. She
wanted to know what I was doing in Paris. And the look she
gave me! As if Paris were banned to me for all eternity.

He gives her a light; she smokes.

ROGER: My father—in all his eighty years I never found out
what he really believed—he was no mystic, heaven knows, but
he always knew what my dead mother was thinking. When he
sold the house, never a doubt that his late wife approved. No
need for her to know that he had messed things up with an inept
bit of speculation, she was an understanding woman, and she
always took his side. A convenient ghost. When we, his sons,
didn't agree with him, it was always she who thought him right.
He was an alcoholic. And he never doubted that she read the
newspaper, too—his newspaper, of course. The long-haired
youngsters: she hadn't lived to see those, but she found them
as dreadful as he did. When he changed his political views,
because they were proving too costly, and when he left the
party, his dead wife left it, too. No doubt about it. I
despised him, found all his communing with the dead
repulsive. . . .

She sits silent, smoking.

ROGER: It was this bench, I'm certain of it. The only one under a street lamp. We didn't feel like sitting in the dark. . . . A year later I got married. You've never seen Ann. I got to know her in Texas, and we have a son, as perhaps you've heard. He's a schoolboy now.

She sits silent, smoking.

ROGER: Say something, Francine, about yourself.

She smokes, her eyes straight ahead. He looks at her.

ROGER: We probably reacted exactly the same way after we parted: you decided you were right, I decided I was right, and all we had left was bitterness. Which is easier on the memory than remorse. Your affair with Roger, mine with Francine, maybe they differ in the degree of their significance, but the dates are the same. . . .

Silence, the heavy traffic is heard, then stillness, then the lighter traffic.

ROGER: If Ann were to walk down this avenue now, she wouldn't be surprised to see me talking to you. She was jealous in the beginning, because I was always justifying myself to Francine, sometimes for hours on end. And she felt it was not her I was contradicting, but you. Poor Ann, it wasn't easy for her. I realized that later. But though I never mentioned your name again, she could still feel your presence, inevitably. . . . Ann's a photographer. . . . She's four years younger than you—that is to say, she was. Now Ann is already somewhat older than you. It's all very strange.

Pause.

ROGER: Incidentally, I did see you again—just once. Almost as close as we are now. I don't think I was mistaken. You were standing on the opposite escalator—it was in Berlin, at the Zoo underground station, in the morning. Can that be right? I was going down, you up, your hand on the railing, alone, and you were looking straight ahead, not exactly radiating cheerfulness, but not unhappy, either. You were deep in thought. Afterwards I felt I'd been quite right not to call out: Francine.

She extinguishes her cigarette against the marble.

ROGER: Or did you recognize me, too?

Pause.

ROGER: I never visited your grave.

A news vendor appears.

NEWS VENDOR: LE MONDE!—

Francine buys a newspaper; it takes some time, since she has to search for change, and obviously has difficulty with the unfamiliar coins without her glasses. At last she finds the right coin, and the news vendor goes off.

ROGER: You bought a newspaper—yes—to have something to read after we'd parted, when you were alone in the hotel bedroom.

She puts on her spectacles.

ROGER: Why did we part?

She glances at the title page.

ROGER: Vietnam . . . You knew how it would end before I did, though you didn't live to see it. But history proved you right. When I read about Chile today, I know exactly what Francine thinks about it.

She turns a page.

ROGER: Ernst Bloch is dead now, too—

She puts the newspaper down on the bench.

ROGER: The future holds nothing but fear.

Pause.

FRANCINE: Shall we go?

He does not move.

ROGER: Later I heard, from other people — and they couldn't have made it up, it can only have come out of your head—I heard I'd been blackmailing Francine for three whole years with threats of suicide.

He puts another cigarette between his lips.

ROGER: Did I do that, Francine?

He flips his lighter and takes the cigarette from his lips before he has lit it.

ROGER: Maybe you went through my drawers, I don't know, but you didn't find a revolver there. I didn't have one. I could always have jumped from the balcony. But I never threatened you with such nonsense. I did go to the Dolomites, that's true, but it wasn't meant as a threat—surely? What else, then? After a party where we'd all been drinking I did once try my hand at being a cat burglar—

He tries to laugh.

ROGER: Was that blackmail?

He throws his cigarette away.

ROGER: I think it's wretched of you, Francine, if that's the way
you told our story: saying I blackmailed you for three years
with threats of suicide.

*She takes a cigarette and at the same time brings out her lighter,
so that he can only look on as she lights her cigarette.*

ROGER: That's how you smoked. And soon we shall start to feel
cold. Later the gendarme will pass by and wonder why we are
not in bed. I've never forgotten how you said: NOUS ATTENDONS
LE MATIN, MONSIEUR! and how he gave a salute. Later still,
when the traffic has stopped, we shall hear an ambulance siren
in the distance. . . .

*The traffic noises are still audible every fifty seconds: though
becoming, not weaker, but shorter, so that the stillness gradually
increases; sometimes only a single bus can be heard.*

ROGER: Say something, Francine!

She smokes, looking straight ahead.

ROGER: For a time—after your death—I toyed with feelings of
guilt. I set you up as my judge, in order to make you speak.
But you didn't listen when I made my confession, and you
looked at me as if it were impossible that I should ever understand. You said nothing—or you just repeated what you said
then, here on this bench. . . . Francine, next year I shall be
fifty, but you are always thirty-three.

*He rises to his feet, without really knowing why he has done so;
she continues to sit, unchanged; he stands with his hands in the
pockets of his coat.*

ROGER: WE SHOULD NEVER HAVE LIVED TOGETHER.

He looks at her:

ROGER: Do you know what I have often thought? That Francine
is in love with her love. And that has nothing whatever to
do with the man she may have met. Francine belongs in the
ranks of the Great Lovers. She loves her bliss, she loves her
fear and her longing and her bitterness, the exaltation of her
yielding, and if the man thinks it has anything to do with him,
he has only himself to blame. Francine is not in love with
herself, I don't mean that. She just loves—like the Portuguese
nun. She loves her love.

He sees that she is not listening to him.

FRANCINE: I shall work.

ROGER: So you said.

FRANCINE: Immerse myself in work.

She extinguishes her cigarette against the marble.

ROGER: That's what you said, and I understood that our parting was decreed, whatever else we would say that night.

She takes her lipstick from her handbag.

ROGER: Why didn't you want to have our child?

She makes up her lips without looking in her pocket mirror; he sits down again on the bench.

ROGER: And you never did have a child. So far as I know. Later I began to suspect that the people in Geneva might have made a mess of things that time.

He looks at her:

ROGER: Francine, was that it?

She puts her lipstick back into her handbag.

FRANCINE: It's two o'clock, Roger, and last night we hardly slept at all. Let's be sensible.

ROGER: That's what you said.

FRANCINE: What is the point of going to the station so early? I can't see why you shouldn't come back to the hotel and rest until it's time for your train.

He is silent.

FRANCINE: What's to happen now with the flat?

He is silent.

FRANCINE: It was you who decided we should part, Roger, last night. For once you showed more courage than I, and for that I am grateful.

ROGER: That's what you said.

FRANCINE: When you've been drinking you can never remember what you said.

ROGER: We had both been drinking.

Pause.

ROGER: What did I say, Francine?

Pause.

FRANCINE: Roger, I'm making no demands.

ROGER: That's what you said.

Pause.

FRANCINE: I can go to live with Marieluise. Anytime. But how do you imagine I can work in her attic?

He is silent.

FRANCINE: Roger, you have never helped me.

He is silent.

FRANCINE: You talk like a landlord. A mere transaction. You say: I'll make you a present of the flat, all it needs is fifteen minutes with a lawyer and the flat is yours, furniture included.

ROGER: That's what I said.

FRANCINE: That's your first thought: lawyers.

He is silent.

FRANCINE: Roger, I have only one request—

ROGER: And I stuck to that: I made no attempt to find out your new address, I didn't appear one day on your doorstep, I didn't ring your bell.

Pause.

FRANCINE: What can I do with six rooms by myself?

He is silent.

FRANCINE: How can you ask what work I shall do? When for a whole year I've been talking about qualifying as a lecturer. You don't take my work seriously.

He is silent.

FRANCINE: Don't worry about me. That's not what I need, your concern. I can read timetables for myself.

He is silent.

FRANCINE: All I need from our flat is my books. Nothing else. The dictionaries in particular. And my clothes.

ROGER: You sent for those.

FRANCINE: If any letters come for me—

ROGER: I always sent them on to Marieluise. As arranged. Some bills as well, perhaps—I don't know. And in the first weeks there were also some telephone calls. I didn't have any number to pass on.

Pause.

FRANCINE: Stop looking at me like a sheepdog.

He is silent.

FRANCINE: You'll go off to Austin, and we'll be relieved, both of us, not to have to prove anything to each other any more.

ROGER: I did go to Austin.

Pause.

FRANCINE: It would be better not to write to each other, Roger, ever. Let's promise that, Roger. Never.

He is silent.

FRANCINE: Roger, you don't need me.

He is silent.

FRANCINE: Who was it who whitewashed the whole flat when you were away in Trieste, all six rooms, standing by myself on the ladder?

He is silent.

FRANCINE: What could I find to do in Austin?

He is silent.

FRANCINE: When we went househunting together, you wanted a large old building with high ceilings, and I agreed with you. Yes, I felt positive that we were not just any old couple.

ROGER: We were Francine and Roger.

FRANCINE: Yes.

ROGER: And so we are.

Pause.

FRANCINE: Roger, I'm getting cold.

He is silent.

FRANCINE: You want me to need you, that's what love means to you. When you're feeling sure of yourself I'm a burden on you. It's when you're feeling unsure that you cling to me, and that's not what I'm here for, Roger.

He is silent.

FRANCINE: There are times when I hate you—

ROGER: That's what you said.

A gendarme comes in and stops before them.

FRANCINE: Nous attendons le matin, monsieur.

The gendarme salutes and goes off.

ROGER: Today, out in Orly—yesterday I didn't even know I'd
be flying to Paris, and this morning, when I had the ticket in
my hand and heard them announce the flight, I was still
unable to tell myself why—it was only in Orly, after arriving
there with no luggage, and when I was sitting in the taxi, that
I felt this mad hope that it might all never have happened,
and that we should meet you and I, in this avenue. . . .
Incidentally, nobody knows I am in Paris. Except Madame
Tailleur. WHAT ARE YOU DOING IN PARIS. This is what I'm
doing: talking to the dead.

*The traffic noise has subsided; now nothing is heard except an
occasional bus, then silence again.*

FRANCINE: Have you another cigarette?

He offers a pack of cigarettes, but no lighter.

ROGER: There are times when I forget you. I'm still wearing
the watch Francine gave me. But it doesn't remind me of you.
And there are places we visited together, Strasbourg, for
instance—the cathedral there reminds me of other cathedrals,
not of Francine. That's how it is sometimes. I wouldn't
confuse your handwriting with anybody else's, were I to see
it, no, but I can't recall what it was like. And your body, your
naked body . . . Oh, that can be agony—in the street, among
the crowds at the traffic lights, I see hair that is your hair
exactly. I know it's not possible, but I don't start walking when
all the others do, I wait until I have forgotten you again.

FRANCINE: Have you a light?

He gives her a light.

ROGER: Sometimes I dream of Francine. You are always
different from the person I know, and usually in the company
of strangers. I try to show you that by stretching out my arms,
I can fly above the roofs. Which is not allowed, of course.
Sometimes you are tender towards me, Francine, in my dreams.
I know that tells me nothing about you, Francine, none of
it is news of you.

Pause.

> Perhaps we parted to show ourselves we could live without each other, and so we could, as long as you were alive.

She looks straight ahead, smoking.

ROGER: Did you go to Hanoi?

She looks straight ahead, smoking.

ROGER: You're tired, Francine.

FRANCINE: Desperately.

ROGER: That's what you said.

She looks straight ahead, smoking.

ROGER: Do you recognize this piece of paper?

He takes a piece of paper from his wallet.

ROGER: How that got into my wallet I've no idea. Like something drawn by a child. Railings. But nothing behind them. Could it be yours? I never saw you drawing.

She extinguishes her cigarette against the marble and again takes her lipstick from her handbag to paint her lips, this time looking into the small pocket mirror; a single bus is heard, then silence.

ROGER: I suppose you heard that I met her once, your Marieluise. At a party. We were standing at a cold buffet, and I probably asked her how Francine was getting on— otherwise I shouldn't have heard the words I did: YOU HAVE NEVER LOVED ANYBODY, ROGER, AND YOU NEVER WILL LOVE ANYBODY. I assumed this judgment came from you, and I left.

She moves her lips to settle her makeup.

ROGER: Would you still say that today?

She puts her lipstick back in her handbag.

ROGER: I know next to nothing about your life after we parted that night. You stayed in Paris. I kept my promise, I never went in search of you, as long as you were alive—

A single car is heard.

FRANCINE: Perhaps that was a taxi.

She has risen to her feet.

FRANCINE: It's two o'clock. Roger, and last night we hardly
   slept at all. Let's be sensible.

She looks at her watch:

FRANCINE: Half past two.

He remains seated and looks at her.

ROGER: Is that the suit you were wearing?

Again a single bus, then silence.

ROGER: When I heard about your operation, the first one—
   the people didn't know I knew Francine Coray, so they spared
   no details—I wrote you a letter, but I didn't send it. I didn't
   dare to, Francine. Then, six months later, there was talk
   of X-ray treatment. . . . That time I did fly to Paris, but out
   there in Orly I knew some white nun would come and tell me
   my presence was not desired.

He puts a cigarette between his lips.

ROGER: I knew Francine was going to die.

He takes the cigarette from his lips.

ROGER: Say something, Francine.

Silence.

ROGER: Incidentally, I'm now alone again. My boy is allowed
   to visit me once a month, and for a fortnight each year. Ann
   is living with another man. It may even have been from me
   that she learned what was once said of me over a cold buffet:
   YOU HAVE NEVER LOVED ANYBODY. . . . A statement like
   that sticks like the mark of Cain.

He lights his lighter, then extinguishes it.

ROGER: I imagine you burned all my letters. I hope so—that
   they're not lying around in that woman's house, Madame
   Tailleur. . . . I haven't burned yours, Francine, though I
   haven't reread them, either. I should be afraid to. Phrases like
   in the Song of Solomon, but now they no longer apply. I've
   put them in a cardboard box, your letters, and sealed them in
   the approved way: with a candle and sealing wax, a drop of
   wax on the string, then a thumb on the hot wax, my finger-
   print as seal.

He lights a cigarette.

ROGER: You were no longer a student when you decided

against having our child, and I'd just passed my fortieth
birthday. I didn't insist on it, no, I certainly didn't. On the
journey to Geneva I asked you again, two or three times. You
never realized how shocked I was by your determination. No,
I didn't let you see that—on the contrary, in fact. I professed
to understand you completely. Maybe my masculine understanding hurt you, I don't know. We were alone in the
compartment, you pulled your coat over your face. But we
were still in love for some time after that—

*The siren of an ambulance is heard in the distance; it comes
closer, though not very close, then fades again.*

ROGER: What had really come between us, long before that,
we didn't talk about at all that night. Not a word. At any
time. Just like any other couple.

*She sits down again on the bench, her handbag under her arm,
ready to leave.*

ROGER: What did we talk about until three in the morning?

Again a single bus, then silence.

ROGER: Once, in one of my dreams, I saw you drawing or
painting. One sheet of paper after another. What you were
drawing so intently I couldn't see. All I saw was one piece of
paper after another, and you, a grown woman, looking
happy, as absorbed as a child, earnest but happy. My presence
didn't upset you. Then I asked you to give me one of your
drawings, you didn't say I could, but you left it to me to
take one or not—and then I woke up. When I turned on the
light, I felt pleased, quite convinced I possessed a drawing
of yours. A sign. I looked for it on the floor, on the table,
in the pockets of my jacket—of course I didn't find anything.

He takes the piece of paper from his coat pocket.

ROGER: I suppose I must have scribbled this myself.

Slowly he crumples the piece of paper.

ROGER: Your silence, Francine—I understood your silence, as
long as you were still alive.

The gendarme comes in exactly as before.

FRANCINE: Nous attendons le matin, monsieur.

The gendarme salutes and goes off.

ROGER: One shouldn't talk with the dead.

She puts the newspaper into her handbag.

FRANCINE: You don't have to accompany me, Roger. Straight on, turn right through the gate, then straight ahead and through the other gate and straight on across the bridge—I know, I can find the way.

He stamps out his cigarette.

ROGER: When I got the news, a printed card, incidentally, with a text chosen by your family—before then it had always seemed possible that we might meet again. Quite by chance. You never sought a meeting, I know that, Francine, and I didn't dare to, and then suddenly the thought that we might see each other again had vanished.

He rises to his feet.

ROGER: But I did accompany you.

She remains seated.

FRANCINE: We did once have a good time together, Roger, a great one. I thought the two of us, you and I, would rethink the whole world. Everything. And there must be something like that: a couple that sees itself as the first couple ever, as the inventor of the idea of couples. Us! The world may be shocked by our arrogance, but it can't hurt us. We have known grace. That's what I believed. And we knew the idea of possession didn't enter into it. Otherwise we should have got married. Once, at the very beginning, you said: There is nothing on this earth that cannot be rethought. And that was the bond between us, Roger. We mustn't let anyone know that we, Roger and Francine, were rethinking the world, including all its dead. The orgies of argument we enjoyed, Roger! And I felt certain we loved more than just each other. You me and I you—all that is interchangeable. So you said! But what brought us together was not interchangeable. Other couples were just man and woman, we decided, and we were that, too, but on top of everything else: as a sort of extra bonus. And you know, Roger, our desperation at that time was never petty—wrong-headed perhaps, but never petty, and we could say terrible things to each other—things we could no longer say now. . . . That's when we bought the big flat. We talked a lot of rubbish, Roger, sometimes I and sometimes you, and sometimes both of us together, but at that time I really did believe I could rethink things, you could rethink things. We weren't dead, Roger, never dead—as we are now.

He looks at her the way one looks at a person who cannot know what he has been saying, and keeps silent.

FRANCINE: And we were proud of each other, you know. We didn't treat each other with kindness or compassion, or expect it, either. We saw each other as two people who had been singled out—yes, I mean that: singled out—me by you and you by me. We moved no mountains, and you often laughed at my optimism. You know, Roger, even in our mistakes we became bolder. We didn't misuse our feelings of tenderness, using them to hide from each other, or to comfort ourselves. . . . Yes, Roger, that's how it was. For a time.

He sits down again.

ROGER: Go on!

FRANCINE: Roger, I'm getting cold.

ROGER: I'm listening.

She is silent.

ROGER: When a memory suddenly finds itself alone in the world, it becomes another story, Francine, a very different one. My need to feel I was in the right—that has vanished since you died, and memory suddenly starts to release other things, now I see you in front of me.

He gazes at her tenderly:

ROGER: You with your narrow forehead and your big teeth, a blond horse with spectacles!

She removes her glasses and puts them into her handbag.

ROGER: And with your eyes like water.

Pause.

ROGER: Incidentally, our flat no longer exists. The house has. been torn down—

Pause.

ROGER: A short while ago I had a conversation with a girl. I hardly know her, an ambitious youngster in search of a scholarship—that's why she came to see me. She had been having an abortion, she said: she felt I ought to know, so I wouldn't think she was always late for appointments. Maybe her frankness embarrassed me, she said, but she was anxious that I should understand her. It was, as she told me: BECAUSE I DON'T KNOW WHO THE FATHER IS. . . .Up till

then it had never occurred to me that our case might have
been the same.

Pause.

FRANCINE: There are times, Roger, when you would like to
slap my face. You don't do it because you know it would mean
you would never see me again.

ROGER: That's what you said, Francine; then you took your
handbag—I could have sworn it was a blue one—

She picks up her white handbag.

ROGER: —and got up.

She rises to her feet.

ROGER: And off we went with scarcely a word: straight on,
turning right through the gate, then straight ahead and through
the other gate, and straight on across the bridge to our white
hotel.

*She is standing, he remains seated, in the manner of a person sitting
alone, hands in pockets, not knowing what to do next, staring
straight ahead into the darkness.*

ROGER: Suddenly—have you ever had this experience?—suddenly
I realize it isn't true, something I had always maintained, which
I had once believed. Suddenly it might all be quite different.
It can seem like an awakening, in the middle of the day. A
sentence I once heard, maybe years ago, comes into my mind,
and suddenly it means something quite different. That is
happening more and more frequently to me now. Without any
reason I can see. I wake up, realizing that a joke I made
yesterday isn't a joke at all. Or I remember some sentence
which for years had aroused my indignation, and to which I
reacted indignantly at the time. But now: I can't really see
why that particular remark upset me so. I don't understand
why I reacted as I did. . . . I don't know if you've ever had
that experience, Francine.

Pause.

ROGER: Do you know, there isn't a single photograph of
Francine that reminds me of you? Except a childhood
photograph: young Francine, looking as I've never seen you
look, together with a large sheepdog.

Pause.

ROGER: Say something!

Pause.

ROGER: Once, after you'd been to Moscow, you spoke about Lenin—how the sight of him in that mausoleum made you feel sick, his wise head empty of thought for the past fifty years. . . . That's the trouble: we live with the dead, and they don't rethink.

Pause.

ROGER: I'm looking forward to a holiday in Iceland with my youngster. I've been telling him how volcanoes and glaciers originate, and now I have to show him that there are such things. He's too old for fairy tales. We're going to Iceland this coming summer. For a fortnight. With a tent and sleeping bags.

Pause.

ROGER: Francine, say something.

FRANCINE: You don't have to accompany me.

ROGER: No, Francine—say something you didn't say then. Something you thought later. Something you would say now—that would set us free of our history, Francine.

Again the siren of an ambulance is heard in the distance; the sound comes nearer, then fades in the opposite direction.

FRANCINE: Roger, I really am cold.

ROGER: Once, months ago, I had the idea that I ought to shoot myself through the head, so that I could hear Francine again.

FRANCINE: And you're cold, too.

He remains seated.

ROGER: Francine, say something.

He suddenly shouts:

ROGER: Say something!

Pause.

FRANCINE: Roger, we've said it all.

ROGER: Have we?

FRANCINE: I told you I would work. Or go to Hanoi, if that were possible, to report on things from the other side.

Pause.

FRANCINE: It was you who decided we should part, Roger. For

once you showed more courage than I, and for that I am grateful.

Pause.

We should never have lived together.

Pause.

How can you ask what work I shall do? When for a whole year I've been talking about qualifying as a lecturer. You don't take my work seriously.

Pause.

Stop looking at me like a sheepdog.

Pause.

You'll go off to Austin, Roger, and we'll be relieved, both of us, not to have to prove anything to each other any more.

Pause.

Roger, you have never helped me.

Pause.

What can I do with six rooms by myself?

Pause.

Roger, you don't need me.

Pause.

Don't worry about me. That's not what I need, your concern. I can read timetables for myself.

Pause.

It would be better not to write to each other, Roger, ever. Let's promise that, Roger. Never.

Pause.

We did once have a good time together, Roger—

ROGER: Go on!

Pause.

FRANCINE: All I need from our flat is my books. Nothing else. The dictionaries in particular. And my clothes.

Pause.

Roger, I'm making no demands.

Pause.

When we went househunting together, you wanted a large old building with high ceilings, and I agreed with you. Yes, I felt positive that we were not just any old couple.

Pause.

That's your first thought: lawyers.

Pause.

Roger, I have only one request: that you never try to find out my new address. Do you promise that? I don't want you appearing one day on my doorstep, ringing my bell.

Pause.

Roger, I'm cold.

Pause.

You want me to need you, that's what love means to you. When you're feeling sure of yourself, I'm a burden on you. It's when you're feeling unsure that you cling to me, and that's not what I'm here for, Roger.

Pause.

What could I find to do in Austin?

Pause.

There are times when I hate you, Roger, but I shall never forget that I once loved you very much.

ROGER: Go on!

FRANCINE: There are times when I hate you—

ROGER: Go on!

FRANCINE: There are times when I hate you—

She stands and looks on as, without haste, he reaches into his coat pocket, as if he were searching for his lighter, and, still without haste, releases the safety catch of a revolver. He does it, not in the manner of a man who is used to it, but as if it had been explained to him.

ROGER: Go on!

FRANCINE: You never loved anybody, Roger, you are not capable of that, and you never will love anybody.

Pause.

ROGER: So that remains.

She looks on as, without haste, he puts the revolver to his temple, as if he were alone; no report, but sudden darkness, then daylight: the bench is empty, the traffic sounds, now loud, are heard again every fifty seconds, the silence between each change very short.